Ski Powder

Martin Epp

Ski Powder
Martin Epp

Illustrated by Mike Peyton

Fernhurst Books

First published 1987 by
Fernhurst Books, 53 High Street, Steyning, W. Sussex

ISBN 0 906754 34 8

Acknowledgements
The author and publishers gratefully acknowledge the assistance of the following
people: Bill Rollo for shooting the Wengen photographs; John Breen for shooting
the photographs on the Wengen to Andermatt traverse; Kath and Mike Peyton,
Huw Alban-Davies and Christine Graves for their helpful advice on the
manuscript; the railways of the Jungfrau region, Wengen, for providing the team
with uphill transport.
   The cover photograph of Andy Blair skiing the powder at Meribel is by Barrie
Smith. The cover design is by Behram Kapadia.

Design by PanTek, Maidstone
Composition by A & G Phototypesetters, Knaphill
Printed and bound in Great Britain by Ebenezer Baylis & Son Ltd, Worcester.

Contents

Introduction

When skiing was first born everyone skied powder, even beginners, but in these days of lifts and piste machines, powder skiing has become the exception. Yet anyone can ski straight through powder, and even beginners can succeed in doing snowplough turns in it. Everyone should have a try.

But there's no doubt that it is the parallel skier who will get the most fun out of powder. He can make interlinked turns using the deep snow as a partner, playing with the centripetal and centrifugal forces and bouncing around on the soft snow as if on a vast feather bed. His technique and balance will improve enormously, as will his enjoyment, while at the same time he will become a safer skier. When you have read this book, I hope you too will be well on the way to getting that much pleasure from the powder.

Before we head for the steep and the deep, a couple of words of warning. Do not ski in powder without a knowledge of avalanche safety (you can read about this in Part Two), and do not follow other skiers blindly: they may not know what they're doing.

Have fun in the powder: piste skiing will never be the same again!

Martin Epp
Andermatt, Switzerland

Part one

TECHNIQUE

1 Getting your ski legs

I always spend the first day of any powder course on piste. This surprises some people, but really there's little point in heading off into deep snow until each person has a reasonable technique. Thereafter we alternate on and off piste, gradually sorting out problems until everyone is ready for the steep and the deep.

In this chapter I want to look at that first day, and teach you a turn that will work in *any* snow conditions. Once you've got it you can ski on piste, fly through powder and even survive in breakable crust. What a turn!

But to begin, as they say, at the beginning.

Preparation

Preparing for the holiday should start at home. Check through all your equipment and have your safety bindings tested. (You can test them yourself but it is likely to be rather inaccurate and you can easily damage your legs.)

When skiing in powder you will be using muscles that you never use normally. If you have no muscles, how can you ski? So do these exercises daily, increasing the number so you finish near to exhaustion.
- Step up onto a chair and down again. Repeat several times.
- Jump over a pile of books. Repeat several times.
- Make some imaginary telemark turns, bending one knee down to the ankle of the other leg, first to one side, then the other.

Other good exercises are swimming, jogging and gymnastics. Sleep well!

UP....... DOWN..... UP.....

Warming up

I was once climbing in Switzerland when a ligament in my finger snapped, leaving me virtually helpless on the rock face. The injury was caused by my limbs being stiff and cold. Eventually I scrambled down, but ever since then I've been keen on warming up before beginning any sport.

In fact, like every other day your skiing day starts in bed. Stretch like a cat, then get out and lie on the floor, arch your back and rock back and forth. While putting your clothes on, stand on one foot and hop about. Do whatever feels good – just loosen up. This may amuse your room-mate, but your body will be in better shape for skiing than his.

At the top of the hill warm up again before your first run. Do all these exercises slowly, and breathe deeply.

●Bend one knee so your ski is vertical behind you, with the tip down. Push so the end of the ski touches your back. Repeat for the other leg.

● Practise a few kick turns (see Chapter 3)

● While stationary, lean right forward like a ski jumper, then right back. Hold your sticks so they're ready to support you if the bindings release.

● Plant the pole by bending your knees and ankles (*not* by stabbing with your arm)

● Stamp both skis into the snow several times using your knees and ankles, not your upper body. Do this faster and faster. Imagine you're on bathroom scales and trying to get the highest reading possible. Not only does this exercise warm up exactly the right muscles, but it also teaches you how to prepare for the turn.

● While stationary, drop into an exaggerated traverse position. Really bend your knees and push your uphill hip forward. When skiing you spend 99 per cent of your time in a traverse – the only exception is a brief moment when you initiate the turn. The drawing shows what to aim for; when you get the position right it feels as though you're about to sit on a bench alongside you. Later I'll explain why you should take up this stance; for the moment just exaggerate it. Then kick turn round and 'traverse' the other way.

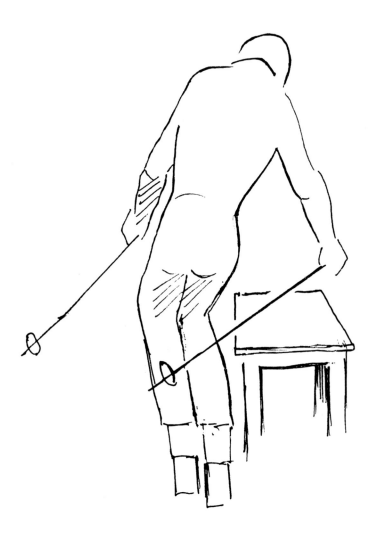

The first run

You're not going to learn much on your first run, so spend it getting used to your skis and boots again. Play with your skis, using only the lower part of your body – your legs. Edge and flatten the skis during the turns. Sideslip for a distance to each side. Don't go too fast; just have fun.

The turn

The picture sequence shows my favourite turn, which will work in any kind of snow. You can also see the turn in motion by flipping the bottom corners of the pages, starting from the back of the book.

• Begin each turn in an exaggerated traverse, upper hip forward, looking down the valley and pressing your shins into the tongues of your boots. Choose a moderate speed.

PREPARING FOR THE TURN

• Now stamp down *hard* with both feet. Note that it's quite wrong to jump up again, and indeed if you do this in powder your skis will simply sink. No, the action is like collapsing and pressing down into a trampoline, which then automatically throws you up. Concentrate on punching down into the snow. This downward movement is jerky, but all the other movements should be smooth.

• At the same time plant the basket close to the ski, at a point midway between the ski tip and your boot. Do this by keeping your elbow at your side and rotating your wrist. The planting is done by the downward movement of your body, not by your arm. Note that when you plant the pole your palm faces forwards, not your knuckles. On a steep slope you'll have to bend your knees more to plant the pole because of the drop – this is perfectly correct.

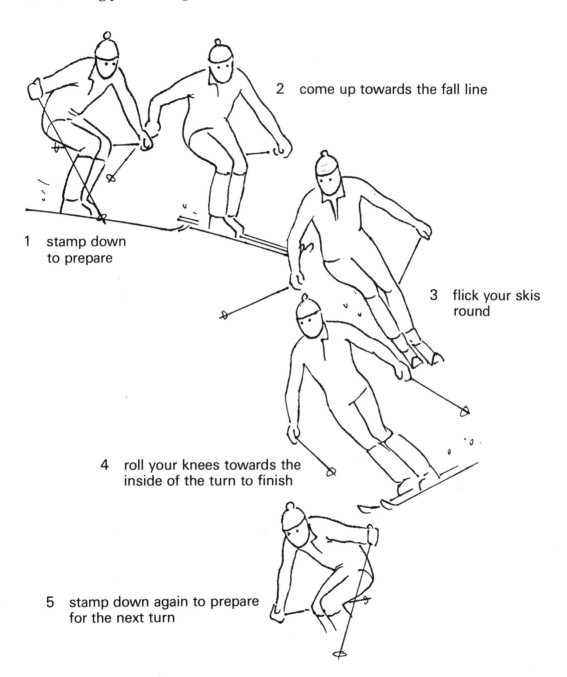

2   come up towards the fall line

1   stamp down
to prepare

3   flick your skis
round

4   roll your knees towards the
inside of the turn to finish

5   stamp down again to prepare
for the next turn

2 come up towards
the fall line

1 stamp down
to prepare

3 flick your skis round

4 roll your knees towards the
inside of the turn to finish

5 stamp down again to prepare
for the next turn

INITIATING THE TURN

- Throw your hips in the direction of the fall line, and throw your weight down the fall line too. In mid-turn your body must be at right angles to the slope. If your weight is back you'll simply accelerate down the fall line.
- *Immediately* rotate your body and roll your knees over to the new traverse position.

COMPLETING THE TURN

- Land gently and bend your knees so you sink low.
- Push the back ends of the skis round.
- Experiment with edging the skis according to the consistency of the snow, the steepness of the slope and your speed.
- While finishing the turn you should feel the thrust of the centrifugal force against the carving skis – a lovely feeling, like a bobsleigh on a banked turn. Finish the turn uphill to control your speed.
- Don't start the next turn until you are in control.

Your entire body apart from your feet should be facing the outside during the whole turn. If you can see the snow spurting off the back of your skis, your body is in the right position. But don't do this too often: you ought to be looking where you are going!

TO SUM UP
1. Down to prepare
2. Up towards fall-line
3. Flick skis around
4. Roll knees to finish the turn
Now you should be down in a traverse position
and preparing for the next turn. Repeat 1, 2, 3 and 4.

While practising, do not be afraid to exaggerate the traverse position and all the movements of the turn. Exaggeration will impress these important actions on your mind. Once you become a good skier you can easily reduce the movement.

THE TRAVERSE

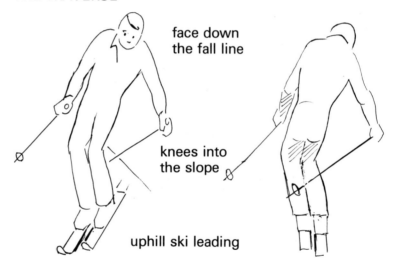

face down
the fall line

knees into
the slope

uphill ski leading

MISTAKES
If you are unsuccessful, your weight is probably too far back. Make sure your knees are bent so there's pressure on your shins. If only I could invent a pill to make people flex their knees and move their weight up and down, they'd learn to ski at the drop of a hat. I'd also be rich!

Check that you aren't edging too much, or the backs will be unable to swing round smoothly. Indeed, you may like to practise turning with your skis almost flat on the snow.

Exercises

You may find the exercises below helpful in sorting out your turn. As you do them , exaggerate each movement – that's the only way to find out if an exercise is going to work. And the more you allow your body to move, the less chance it has to be stiff and the more you will be able to learn.

Try to use your skis like a monoski at all times: aim to keep them together with equal weight on each. This is good practice for powder: if your weight is on one ski in soft snow it will sink and you'll soon lose your balance.

Do each exercise on piste and at a variety of speeds, but don't go too fast to begin with. Indeed, try making the turns very slowly. You can only succeed in making a slow turn if you exaggerate the movements and do them precisely. (Remember to keep the skis flat when turning slowly.)

• Concentrate on your legs. Try to use them alone to keep your balance.

• From a standing start ski forward and make one turn. As you pass through the fall line, exaggerate the new traverse position so you continue to turn uphill until you eventually stop and then start to slide backwards. Check the slide, then repeat the turn in the opposite direction. This exercise gives practice at finishing your turns, which is vital on steep slopes. Think in terms of swinging the backs of the skis round, rather than steering them. It should almost feel as though the backs are overtaking you.

• Schuss down a gentle slope planting alternate poles. Remember to begin with the poles angled back, with their points behind you and your hand near your hip. Now, without moving your arm, rotate one wrist so the knuckles face backwards. This will swing the basket forward. At the same time bend your knees and ankles to plant the pole. The basket will land naturally, a short distance in front of your boot. Now extend your legs and prepare to plant the other pole.

• Stand still with the middle of the skis on top of a bump and the tips and backs of the skis in the air. Sink down to plant the downhill pole as described above, skis tight together, then push up with your legs and 'throw' your weight in the direction of the fall line.

The skis will start to pivot around the planted pole. Keep your hips and chest facing down the valley and drop down into the new traverse position to finish the turn.

Do not rotate your outer arm while all this is going on – at the end of each turn the outer pole must point uphill, not down the valley.

• Practise the same movement without the help of a bump, exaggerating all the time.
• Traverse across the slope and practise rolling your knees downhill. Each time you release the edges you'll sideslip a bit, so roll your knees back to reset the edges. Repeat several times.
• Try making long turns on a gentle slope. Give yourself plenty of time to re-establish the traverse position before beginning the next turn. Then try linking the turns.
• Use a similar technique to make a long turn in a series of 'bites'. Begin the turn as usual, then push, push, push the skis around by rolling your knees. Don't rotate your body; all the action must come from your knees and ankles.

• Make some short turns, and imagine your heels are swinging around like windscreen wipers. Try to make the backs of your skis throw snow to the outside of each turn (you may have been showered like this when someone did an emergency stop above you). Occasionally, have a look at the snow flying: this is good practice for powder, where you need to take up an extreme traverse position facing the deep snow that you're pushing away on each turn. Feel the force and counter-force.

Now try to look ahead as you ski while keeping the mental image of the snow flying off the backs of the skis. This should keep you in the right position, while preventing your colliding with something hard.

• Try this relaxation exercise on an easy slope. Make your body as floppy as possible – in fact ski as though you're drunk (this exercise is always more successful after lunch). Feel your knees automatically absorbing every bump. If you can ski this well when you're totally relaxed, why bother to tense up?

• Once more, exaggerate all movements. Play around to see what happens. Try bending your knees a ridiculous amount and then skiing with straight legs. Notice how much stronger you feel when you're low down, because your centre of gravity is low. Remember: if you can't bend your knees, you can't ski.

INTO THE POWDER

If you've resisted the lure of the powder this long, you should be feeling strong and balanced on your skis. Here's a final exercise to consolidate your turns, and give you an easy introduction to off-piste skiing.

● Find a place where some deep snow lies just off the edge of the piste. If the powder slopes up from the piste, as at the edge of a gulley, so much the better.

Ski towards the powder, begin the turn on-piste but complete it in the deep snow, smashing the backs of your skis around. Finally traverse back onto the piste again. Feels good, doesn't it?

2   Faultfinder

Most people have a pretty good idea of what's wrong with their skiing. 'If only I could get my weight forward . . .' they moan, or 'I know my legs are straight, I just can't make them bend'.

The faultfinder section which follows is designed to help you get away from your pet problem. Treat it just like the troubleshooting chapter of your car manual: I hope it soon has you firing on all four cylinders.

Fault	Comments	Remedy
Reaching too far forward to plant the pole.	This forces you to bend at the waist and to swivel the wrong shoulder forwards. You get a great view of your ski tips, and the person behind gets a great view of your bottom.	Swing the basket forward with your wrist, not with your arm. Pull your shoulder back at the same time.
Bending forward at the waist.	This upsets your balance mechanism. Good balance comes from your feet – there should be no movement above the waist.	Push your knees forward and rotate your hips so your pelvis points down the valley. Look ahead, not at your skis. Plant the stick as above, knuckles facing backwards. Try skiing with a book on your head (preferably not this one).
You ski stiffly.	You may be skiing too fast. Skiing stiffly will throw you off balance, like a car without springs.	Slow down. Choose easier terrain. Exaggerate the down movement at the beginning of each turn. If the problem persists, do some more warm-up exercises. Play around with all the movements, even a few of the wrong ones.
Your position is too high with your downhill leg straight.	If you don't bend your knees and ankles you can't ski.	Check that your boots allow you to angle your lower leg forwards. Better still, rake the boot forwards so it forces you into the right position.

Fault	Comments	Remedy
Skis too far apart.	This can give stability on piste to beginners but will cause all sorts of problems later, especially in powder.	Don't try to force them together. The main problem is your traverse position. Push your upper hip forward and the skis will come together automatically.
Too much weight on the upper ski.	You are leaning into the slope too much. Usually you are too far back, with the skis apart.	Go back to an exaggerated traverse position by bringing your hips forward. This will distribute the weight correctly on the skis.
Skis apart when going down to prepare the turn.	This is usually an old habit from doing stem christianias.	Concentrate on getting rid of this habit by checking that you are in a good traverse position before beginning a turn, and force your feet together as you push down to initiate the turn.
You fall outwards halfway through the turn.	Your upper body is rotating with the turn.	After initiating the turn face towards the outside of the turn and lower your body position.
You fall backwards after starting the turn.	You are extending forwards towards the ski tips, instead of towards the fall line. Just going forward and up will not cause a turn.	After the preparation extend towards the fall line and concentrate on flicking the skis round to the new direction.

Fault	Comments	Remedy
Weight back.	The first part of the turn goes well, but you then shoot downhill with ever-increasing speed.	Once again, check your traverse position. Pushing the upper hip forward forces your weight forward. As you turn, imagine you're a ski jumper. Push down, then explode up and forwards towards the fall line. Try to get your nose over the tips of your skis. At the same time throw the backs round, landing in the new traverse position. Finish by allowing the backs of the skis to skid round.
You get going too fast and scare yourself.	You're sitting back too much. You may be skiing terrain that is too steep and difficult.	Begin in a shallow traverse. Pull your hips forward and slow down by finishing each turn (make sure the skis point almost uphill before you begin the next turn). Look further ahead to see what's coming and plan where you're going to turn. A good skier may look as if he is travelling more or less straight down the fall line. That's because you can't see his skis beneath the snow — *they* are across the fall line though his upper body is pointing downhill. The motion is like sitting on a chairlift and rotating your skis from side to side like a windscreen wiper.

Fault	Comments	Remedy
Your downhill shoulder is pointing forward at the end of the turn.	Your upper body is rotating the wrong way, dragging your hips with it.	Look where you're planting the basket at the beginning of each turn, then look at the backs of the skis as the turn is completed. Relax your upper body and put all your strength in your legs.
Your hands come up to shoulder height when you get nervous.	This often forces your outer shoulder forward.	Ski for a while with the insides of your elbows touching your sides.
Bus driver position.	You are in a sitting position facing forward towards the ski tips, skis apart and steering the skis with your entire body strength.	Push your uphill hip forward. As you begin to turn flick your hips round to the new traverse position *immediately*. It's impossible to sit back when your body is twisted; looking down the valley.
Tripping up halfway round the turn.	You fall outwards because your skis catch in soft snow.	Exaggerate the preparation of each turn by stamping both skis into the snow. The reaction will help lift you out of the snow to initiate the turn. Land *gently* in a good traverse position so you don't get thrown off balance. The only jerky movement is the push down to initiate each turn.
The skis are hard to turn.	The skis may be too stiff. You are edging them too much.	Practise with nearly flat skis on an easy piste, then experiment in various kinds of snow off piste.

Fault	Comments	Remedy
You are off balance.	Your arms are usually waving all over the place. The lower part of your body is too stiff.	Look further ahead. Ski on easier slopes doing a lot of turns. Practise straight runs over uneven ground, but not too fast. Lower your centre of gravity.
You are frightened of bumps.	You don't know how to pick your way through them. You are going too fast and you are out of control.	You can usually find an easier route on the side of the mogul-field. If not, stand still on top of each bump. Turn around the steep part of the bump and stop on top of the next bump down.
Poor control of speed.	It isn't that your skis are too fast! You are pointing them towards the fall line too much.	Ski across the slope rather than down it. Get low before starting the turn, and finish the turn by going very low again and turning uphill.
Nothing wants to work any more.	You are too tense. You forgot the preparation before the turn. You are too stiff.	Get more relaxed by exaggerating all the movements, especially the preparation before the turn. That means you have to stamp your skis hard into the ground, then turn.

3 First steps off-piste

Before you head off into the unknown, make sure you can do really good kick turn. If you find yourself stuck on a really steep slope, or frightened in breakable crust, or injured, it may be the only sure way to turn round.

- Position yourself exactly across the fall line, and stamp your uphill ski into the snow to form a steady platform.
- Plant your uphill pole above your skis, 30 cm (12 in) in front of your boots.
- Face downhill and plant the other pole near the backs of your skis, and uphill of them. (This will stop you tripping over the pole in the middle of the kick turn.) Now you're ready to swivel your downhill ski round to point the other way.
- Pull your downhill boot back, then swing it forward so the back of the ski digs into the snow about 30 cm (12 in) behind the tip of the other one. Your downhill ski is almost vertical at this point.
- Now swing your leg round so the downhill ski lies parallel to the uphill one, but pointing the other way. Charlie Chaplin would have been proud of you.

● Finally kick the uphill ski forward so it swings around and joins its partners. Keep the ski horizontal on its journey (try to avoid letting the tip point upwards).

You are now facing in the new direction, in exactly the same spot as you started. Practise the manoeuvre until you can repeat it four times in a row without sliding in any direction. Then try it on a steep slope.

NOW FOR THE FUN BIT!

Although the turn we have been practising on piste works perfectly in powder, you may like to bear a few key points in mind.

Don't sit back Most people believe you have to lean or sit back in powder. I think this may be out of fear that the tips will nosedive, or because photos of powder skiers seem to show them well back. All I can say is that it is absolutely fatal to sit back – stay in the same position you were using on piste. The tips *won't* submerge, and the photos are an optical illusion. (You can't judge the skier's body position from a photo because his skis are under the snow – believe me, he's not sitting back if he is a good skier.)

The only time you do need to lean back is when you leave the piste and first hit soft snow, because the deceleration throws you forward.

To see the turn
in action flip
the pages from
the back

And finally, even if you *do* manage to ski sitting back there is an enormous leverage on your knees. The chances are you will damage them; at the very least you will tire quickly in this position. Downhill racers may lean back to gain speed, but they pay for it in knee trouble later.

Don't jump up To turn in powder you need to have your skis unweighted when you begin to turn. Many people try to do this by sinking down slowly, then jumping up. Don't! All that happens is that your boots sink, your edges catch, and you're tripped up just at the critical moment when you should be flying. The right motion is more like loading a spring – stamp down fast with both feet as you plant the pole, and trust the snow to throw you up 'on the rebound'. With your skis unweighted you can initiate the turn so much more easily.

Don't head off too far If possible, do a few turns on piste, then a few in powder, then back on piste again. And do try to find good snow; as a powder puppy (an apprentice powder hound) don't go straight into breakable crust or you risk putting yourself off for life.

Digging out skis

Inevitably you'll fall in the deep snow and your skis will come off. They can be hard to find.

• First study your track carefully before getting up. Generally the lost ski will be found higher than you think; on the other hand it can also glide forward under the light powder. If it does you can generally see its track by a faint indentation.

• If you still have one ski on, take it off and use it to cut the snow diagonally across your tracks, first one way, then the other.

• If you've lost both skis, use the handle end of one pole to cut diagonals in the snow. It's ineffective to jab with the pole.

4 Skiing various types of snow

Snow is infinitely variable – that's what makes skiing so interesting! You need to be able to recognise different snow types and react to them as you zoom from one to another.

Powder on a steep slope

Powder is snow that can't be made into a snowball. And powder is what skiing is all about. Once you've whooshed downhill with the snow flying over your head you'll never be the same again.

On a steep powder slope you can't afford to spend much time in the fall line. In other words, you have to get your tips quickly through the fall line and round to the new traverse.
- Prepare yourself by collapsing down into an exaggerated traverse position. This really loads the spring.
- Allow yourself to be 'thrown' all the way up and round the turn. At the same time force your weight forward – in the middle of the turn your body should be at right angles to the slope. If it isn't, you're sitting back and your speed will increase – fast!
- Simultaneously whip the skis around rapidly, almost jumping them round.
- Land, and collapse down low into the new traverse position.
- Stay down until you're under control, then use this position as a platform for the next turn.

Although it's very satisfying to link dozens of turns, if you get going too fast or are out of phase with yourself, stop and think. Go back to the exaggerated movements.

FLIP

COMMON MISTAKES

Staying too long in the 'down' position at the beginning of the turn Stamp down hard, then begin the turn immediately.

Remaining in the 'up' position and flying straight down the fall line If you don't throw your weight forward you'll sit back and the skis will take charge.

Going too fast Finish each turn! There's no need to push the backs round, they'll slide enough on their own if you force yourself into the new traverse position. But do allow the skis to swing almost across the fall line. On a really steep slope I almost stop after each turn.

Landing too stiffly Land softly, or you will be thrown off balance.

One ski sinks Keep equal weight on both skis.

Skis apart Keep your skis together, like a monoski.

Deep powder

You need a steep slope to overcome the resistance of deep powder, so watch out for avalanches (see Part two).

● Your skis will hardly move, so you only need to make shallow linked turns. In other words ski the fall line, changing direction very little.

● It still helps to make the bouncing movement, but you don't need to bring your skis up to the surface on each turn.

● If your skis are too stiff they will tend to bore into the snow, forcing you to lean back (bad!). Skis that are too soft will hardly move.

Wet snow

Heavy snow, slush, mashed potatoes – call it what you will – is the result of a wet snowfall or rain on old snow. You often find this late in the season; mind you don't ski into any fish!

Avoid skiing steep slopes or you will start a slide. Also check your bindings: the risk of breaking an ankle is high because your skis are held tightly in the snow.

• Heavy snow isn't springy, so you can't get the normal bounce effect by pushing down in the preparation stage. Indeed, too much up and down movement pushes the skis deeper into the porridge. So to start the turn concentrate on coming up very hard, leaning forward down the fall line.

• Each turn will take a long time, so go into it as slowly as possible. Just say to yourself 'The impossible takes a little longer'.

• Experiment with different degrees of edging. You're aiming for long smooth turns, so the skis want to be fairly flat. Indeed, with severe edging you can't turn at all. On the other hand, with no edging you'll slide sideways, so play around with your knees until you feel things are right. Flicking the skis round is not really possible: you have to use force.

COMMON MISTAKES
Skiing with your feet too far apart It's very difficult to control each ski individually.

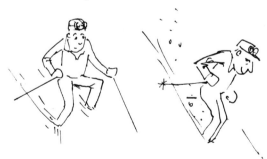

Poor control of speed It's no good going too fast or too slowly, so experiment until you find a speed that works. Waxing your skis is particularly helpful in deep snow.

FLIP

Spring snow

Spring snow is old snow which has crystallised as a result of getting wet, has frozen overnight and has finally been cooked by the sun. The result is a thin layer of beautiful, loose, wet crystals on a firm base. It's an excellent surface to ski on, being rather like sugar or wet salt. Your skis don't sink in much and you can get a firm grip on the hard base, but you can slide the skis in the soft upper layer. Your standard turn works beautifully and, even if your technique isn't up to much, you can get away with murder. No wonder the locals wait for the spring to go skiing.

Unfortunately these ideal conditions are very short-lived. They last only for an hour or two in the morning, usually on a south-facing slope. Do not ski this type of snow once your skis are breaking through, because this will cause deep ruts that spoil the snow for the next day. These particular conditions are also prone to avalanche.

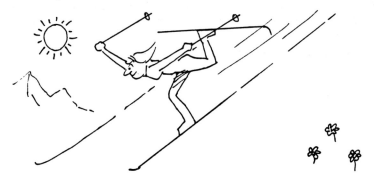

Breakable crust

Your technique needs to be very good indeed to handle breakable crust. In these conditions the top layer of the snowfield has a crust, formed either by the sun or the wind, which breaks when you ski on it. There's soft snow underneath.

There are two main problems: you can't swing the backs of the skis around at the end of each turn, and the texture of the crust usually varies, sometimes being hard enough to support you, and sometimes so powdery that you sink.

It helps to have soft skis because they automatically surface at the tips without your having to lean back.

• Punch down hard to initiate the turn. You will break through the crust, but the reaction will then throw you up and clear of it.

• Once above the crust change the direction of the skis and roll your knees inwards.

• Land very gently.

• The trick now is to edge the skis according to your speed; this is critical, and can only be learned by experiment.

• Now give another hard stamp with both feet to begin the next turn.

If the crust becomes more difficult or the slope gets steeper, emphasise the movements until you're virtually making a jump turn: stamp down, allow yourself to be thrown in the air and spin your skis round breaking through the crust on landing.

If conditions are worse than that, carry your skis.

COMMON MISTAKES

Your first mistake was going onto the crust in the first place.

Stiff skis If your skis have stiff tips they won't work.

Landing too hard If you land hard your skis make a hole, stop, and trip you up.

Going too fast Slow down by choosing the correct angle down the slope. Try to land pointing in the required direction, because it's difficult to skid the backs round any further.

FLIP

Crud

By crud I mean snow that has been chopped up by other skiers. It may then freeze. The skis are thrown around by the ruts as you ski over them.
- You need slightly more speed than usual to help you smash through the uneven snow.
- Keep your centre of gravity low by bending your knees.
- Put all your strength into your legs: if you're too relaxed your skis will vibrate all over the place.

COMMON MISTAKES
Being too passive You have to attack the slope.
Sitting back too far Don't!
Not facing out round the turn Make sure you move quickly to the new traverse position.

Ice

Often the sun melts the snow on a south-facing slope, which then freezes to produce ice. Ice can also form on piste where people have turned a lot.

You may be able to avoid the problem by restricting your skiing to north-facing slopes. But if you are faced with ice, stiff skis and sharp edges are helpful.

- Keep a lookout and avoid ice patches if you can.
- If you hit ice don't fight against it: simply traverse across, letting the skis sideslip until you find a patch of loose snow at the bottom. (There always is one, even if it's further away than you'd like.)
- Now let the skis grip on this snow, or turn on it.

COMMON MISTAKES
Tensing up Don't go stiff and fight the ice, because this throws you off balance. It also has little effect: you'll still slide sideways till you hit soft snow, which then trips you up.
Being caught out Do look far enough to spot icy patches, and watch for snowy areas to turn on.

FLIP

5 Skiing bumps

Although you won't normally find bumps off-piste, I've included a few hints on handling moguls so you can see that this technique really is universal.

Bumps form when people turn at the same place again and again. They're found on steep slopes and there is no limit to their height. On Tortin in Verbier, for example, the moguls are so big that if you stand in a trough you can't see over them.

Technique

- Prepare your turn on the uphill side of the mogul. As you ski over it, the bump 'loads the spring' for you by pushing your skis up.
- Initiate the turn by throwing your weight forward down the fall line. Then drop into the hollow between the bumps and lower your weight – it feels as though you're hiding behind the mogul like a mouse.
- Finish the turn in the traverse position and edge your skis on the uphill side of the next bump down.
- You can either turn round the bump, or go across to the next one.
- You can control your speed by lowering your weight (get really low), by edging your skis in the valley or by doing a check turn on the uphill side of each bump. Try to avoid flying from bump to bump like a demented pogo stick.

COMMON MISTAKES
Going too fast Do a check turn (swing uphill) before each full turn.

Leaning back too far You'll simply accelerate down the fall line. Throw yourself forward into each turn.

Taking the wrong route You slither down the back of each bump, scraping yet more snow off them. The problem is you're frightened to go down into the hollow, just as many people are reluctant to 'let go' when skiing over any icy patch.

Not planning your route Look at least two moguls ahead, and try to almost stop on each one. Once you're on a wrong line it's practically impossible to correct it, so turn uphill, stop and begin again.

6 Bad visibility

In really poor light the best thing is to take up another sport. Water skiing can be fun.

Your natural reactions are to tense up and to lean back because you can't trust your eyes and you're afraid of hitting something. Your legs must become antennae so you can react to bumps and keep your balance.

Head for the tree line, where there is more definition and, with luck, a few shadows. It may pay to ski low down the mountain or near the top, since there is often a band of cloud halfway up.

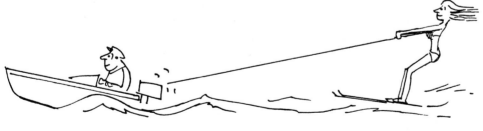

FLIP

Part two

MOUNTAINCRAFT

FLIP

1 Equipment

If you want to go ski touring or ski langlauf, you'll need special equipment. In this book I'm assuming you want to remain a downhill sker, and are planning to ski on and off piste using your normal equipment. Let's look at a few modifications and wrinkles that will make life easier and safer as you move off piste.

Skis

Buy skis according to your height, weight and skiing ability. Ask friends, your instructor or a guide which skis work well off piste.

LENGTH
If the skis are too short you'll have problems with forward/backward balance. The edges are short so they won't grip well on ice, and the skis will be more difficult to control going straight ahead. However, short skis are easy to turn.

If the skis are too long they won't turn well, though they are steadier on a straight fast run.

In powder use the longest skis you can manage because these give the best bearing surface. The taller, heavier and more expert you are the longer the skis you can handle.

FLEXIBILITY
If the skis are too soft they will bend too much in soft snow and you'll find yourself skiing on their middle sections. They will be slow and will grip badly, but you can turn easily.

If the skis are too stiff they'll dig into soft snow and make you cartwheel. They're also hard to turn.

It's most important that the shovel (the tip of the ski and the lead up to the tip) is soft and gently curving. Then when you turn, the shovel takes up a nice curve and pushes you round. The ends of the skis should be as flexible as the tips.

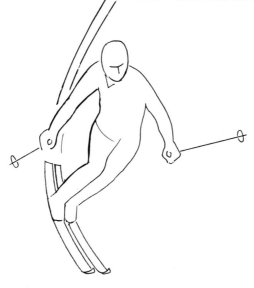

WAX

Nowadays there's no need to rub wax on from a small cake, because modern ski bottoms are good in most types of snow. But you'd be amazed how much easier it is to turn on skis that have been hot waxed recently. This is not done to make the skis faster (though they are) but to help them slide sideways. You're then less likely to catch an edge.

EDGES

Even for off piste work, keep your edges sharp or your technique will suffer. You can either attack them yourself with a file, or use the excellent machines in the shops. Each edge should be cut at a right-angle, with no burrs.

FLIP

Bindings

Use any recognised safety binding, but make sure you understand how to adjust it.

Check the forward release by putting on one ski. Face a wall with the ski tip against it. Step forward with your free foot, then jerk forward in the same way with your ski foot, being careful not to damage your achilles tendon. If the binding doesn't release, adjust it.

To check the sideways release ask a friend to kick the toe of your boot sideways. You should come out of your bindings easily.

You need the same settings for powder as you do on piste. Bear in mind your ability – if you're jumping around like a horse you'll need to set your bindings so the skis stay on. Good skiers can have hair-trigger bindings; skill not only makes skiing easier, it makes it safer.

I'm often asked if people should wear safety straps, and I always say 'no'. This is because you want your skis to come off if you are in an avalanche, and you don't want to be hit by an attached ski if you tumble in powder. Don't worry, there are plenty of ways to find lost skis.

Boots

Your boots are more important than your skis. Often when looking at a class of beginners I know that their boots are going to stop them skiing properly. In fact a good modern boot can be adjusted to the correct angle of forward lean, and can even be canted (to allow for people who are knock-kneed or bow-legged) so the skis remain flat on the snow.

Don't pad out your boots with thick socks. The inner boot should be a snug fit all round and the sole must be a mirror image of your foot. This gives you 'feel' and control when you're playing with the edges, and you are less likely to get cramp in your feet. your boots should definitely not hurt when you're skiing, and it's most important that they don't cut off the blood supply to your feet.

Sticks

Adjustable sticks are a great help. In any case they should be strong as it's surprisingly difficult to ski home with a broken pole. Mine can be made into sounding rods to find people buried beneath the snow.

It's important that your hands do not stay attached to your poles in an avalanche. Sabre grips are my favourite way round this, followed by loops which release. The best thing to do with fixed loops is to cut them off.

Surprisingly, your baskets don't sink into soft snow much when you're turning, so a big area is not essential.

FLIP

An off-piste back pack

Essential	Useful
spare goggles	sounding rod
mittens	whistle
woolly hat	map
shovel (for digging people out or making a snow cave)	compass
	skins (so you can walk unhill to an injured person)
piste map	
wool scarf	spare clothes
pliers	bandage
screwdriver	straps (in case you have to carry two two pairs of skis)
tape	
wire	avalanche bleeper
pencil	radio transmitter/receiver
notepaper	thermal blanket
rescue flag (1m or 2m across, red with white ring)	food
	pain-killing pills

Pack

If you're skiing off piste your need a back pack. In the list of contents above some of the items are essential, though it would be nice to have them all.

Insurance

Before you leave the piste check that your insurance will cover you for rescue and medical treatment on unpatrolled areas.

2 The party

Never, never ski alone off piste. Four to six people is a good size for the group, then you can send for help, transport casualties and so on. There's also more chance of hearing a new joke.

Ideally the leader should be a qualified local guide, who may also act as your instructor. The ski school, tourist office or mountaineering school will help you find someone suitable. Note that ordinary ski instructors are not qualified in off-piste safety, though they can usually ski beautifully in deep snow.

If you can't afford a guide, then take along someone knowledgeable whose mountaincraft is good and who is well acquainted with the area.
- He or she should obtain an avalanche report from local sources or by phoning for the weather forecast or avalanche bulletin (look under W and A in the phone book).
- He should tell you all where you're going, and arrange a rendezvous for anyone who may get lost.
- He should also organise a central place to phone in case people end up in different resorts.
- For longer trips, he should tell someone where you're going and when you ought to be back.
- He should designate one good skier to come last in the group.

When skiing in a party spread out a bit so you don't collide. Also if there is an avalanche the whole group is less likely to be buried when spread out.

Don't ski towards each other (head-on collisions can kill). On the other hand don't lose sight of your friends; the leader should always be able to stop and see the tail-ender.

FLIP

3 Finding the best snow

Wind ruins powder, or blows it away. So unless it has snowed very recently you will need to look for powder in sheltered places:
- In the lee of the mountain (work out the prevailing wind – usually it is from the west or south-west).
- In the lee of ridges.
- Among the trees (but take care not to disturb wild animals).
- In bowls.

Direct sunlight also wrecks powder. If you want to ski in the sun, follow it around the mountain. In the morning ski on east-facing runs, and in the evening move to west-facing slopes.

The powder lasts longest on north-east, east and south-east facing slopes because they receive only the weak morning sunlight. Even north-facing slopes are warmed by slanting rays from the evening sun.

Taking a line

Once you have found a good area, you need to choose a good line (route) down it. This is an important part of the test we give potential group leaders. Having sidestepped through bushes, climbed over barbed wire and attempted to walk up vertical faces to reach virgin snow, the party won't be best pleased if the leader then takes them through narrow gulleys or makes long traverses. They'll expect a good wiggle in powder for their pains.

To take a good line the leader should:
- End up at the chosen point. It's perfectly in order to walk

up to keep on good snow, but having to walk out of a cul-de-sac is a sign of bad navigation.
- Know the mountain. Study a map, to check you're skiing in the right area.
- Make use of vantage points to plan the next part of the route.
- Aim for the best snow. Avoid breakable crust, rocks and narow gulleys. If you must ski through a gulley, one side will usually have better snow because it is sheltered from the wind or sun.
- Take a safe route. Avoid skiing on or beneath a cornice (overhang). Think hard about avalanches (see Chapter 4). Make sure you stop well short of cliffs, so that anyone falling won't go over.

FLIP

• Choose an easy place for each turn. In varied snow, for example, go over the crust until you can turn in powder. Look for natural little bumps to turn on: you should be able to differentiate between rounded humps and rocks covered with a thin layer of snow. If you can't find a reasonable spot, consider stopping and doing a kick turn rather than risking most of the party falling.

• Pick the right speed for the slope, and for the visibility. If you ski too fast the people behind have either to go at a dangerous speed or lose you. So choose a speed the weakest skier can cope with.

• Ski the mountain in sections, stopping each time the tail-ender is about to go out of sight. This is safe, gives the weaker brethren a chance to catch up and will save the leader walking long distances uphill to help someone in trouble.

• Avoid making long traverses across wide virgin slopes. This is not only boring, but messes up the snow for the next party – or for your own group on their next run. Be neat with your 'handwriting in the snow'.

Occasionally it's good for morale to let the team ski down first, otherwise they may get the idea that you're hogging the fresh snow. But do make sure they know where to stop, and check that there's no cliff for them to fall over.

4 Avalanches

My father was a hut keeper. (He also made skis, Epp Skis, which were used in the Olympic Games.) One day I was skiing with him from the hut towards our home when the whole slope began to avalanche. Father was ahead and all I had time to do was ski over to a group of small trees, fall through the soft snow and hang on to their roots. The avalanche roared over the top, burying me. Eventually I got my head out and spotted my father 500 metres below, looking over a cliff. He obviously thought I'd been swept over it, and was overjoyed when I shouted 'hullo'.

I've been in four avalanches, and many of my friends have been killed in them. Whole books have been written on the subject, and avalanche research is going on all the time. In this chapter all I can hope to do is open your eyes to the main dangers, advise you on how to survive in an avalanche, and give a few hints on what to do if you have to dig someone out.

Types of avalanche

Loose snow avalanches start from a small patch of snow and grow as they roll downhill. They're particularly common in the wet snow conditions found in spring and summer.

Slab avalanches occur when a huge plate of snow breaks off and slides down the mountain. Either the whole slope slides over the ground or, more likely, the top layers slide over the fixed lower layers. There is usually a frightening 'crack' as the slide begins. The main reason for this happening is poor adhesion between the layers, caused by wind (which makes the slab) or a long period of weathering. When new snow falls on the old snow it doesn't stick well.

FLIP

Is an avalanche likely today?

An expert will consider dozens of factors before deciding if a slope is safe. For the beginner it is best to concentrate on the geography of the slope, and give only secondary consideration to the snow structure or other factors like the weather. Here are some pointers to bear in mind.

SLOPE DIRECTION
Windslab avalanches are the greatest danger. When the wind carries snow across a ridge or col, it forms a vortex on the lee side and deposits layers of unstable snow on these slopes. The large masses of snow that fall in the Alps are deposited by winds from the south and west. For this reason you can expect to find windslab conditions on north- and east-facing slopes. These are also the slopes that offer the best powder snow conditions which, of course, attract the skier! Ninety per cent of avalanche incidents occur on north- and east-facing slopes.

   The remaining ten per cent occur on south- and west-facing slopes, and are usually triggered by people crossing them too late in the day in the spring.

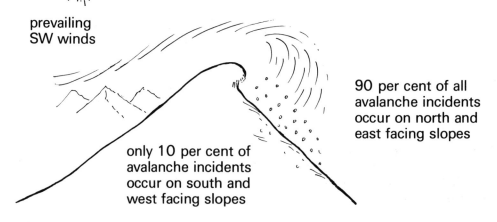

prevailing
SW winds

90 per cent of all avalanche incidents occur on north and east facing slopes

only 10 per cent of avalanche incidents occur on south and west facing slopes

SLOPE GRADIENT

The greatest risk of avalanche occurs on slopes with gradients of between 28° and 45°. A slope steeper than 45° loses its snow during a snowfall and a slope shallower than 28° is not steep enough to cause a slide.

Ski sticks can be used to check the gradient of a slope. Place one stick vertically in the snow. Keep the other horizontal and slide it down the first until its basket hits the snow. If the handles touch the gradient is 45°. If the horizontal stick is half way up the vertical stick, the gradient is 28°.

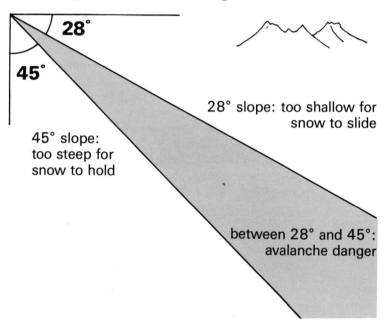

28°

45°

45° slope:
too steep for
snow to hold

28° slope: too shallow for
snow to slide

between 28° and 45°:
avalanche danger

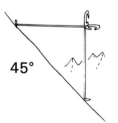

28°

45°

ASSESSING THE TERRAIN

- A forest is usually safe, except open forest such as larch.
- A ridge is usually safe because an avalanche will divide and pass each side of it.

FLIP

● Ground with big boulders is safe as long as it is not completely covered.

● Undulating ground is less dangerous, but watch out for the higher slope above.

● A gulley is unsafe, particularly if it is below a wide steep slope. An avalanche may roar down the slope and funnel through the gulley.

● A cliff at the foot of a slope is unsafe, as you may be swept over it.

● A slope which has uncut grass beneath the snow is very dangerous, as the snow cannot stick to the ground.

● Avalanche fences indicate lethal slopes. In any case, it is illegal to ski through these fences.

● A steep, wide slope is often unsafe.

● A cornice (overhang) is bad news. Never ski beneath one or you may take away its foundation and make it fall on you. Of course, never ski *on* a cornice.

• If you see a fresh avalanche on a slope that faces in the same direction as your own, it indicates that *your* slope may slip too. Don't ski it.
• Terraced slopes hold much better than smooth ones.

ASSESSING THE SNOW

There are no good rules of thumb for assessing the snow. However, I'm so often asked about the safety of various snow types I've included a few thoughts here.

More than 30cm (12in) of fresh snow is unsafe. With 50 – 80cm (20 – 30in) there is great danger. 80 – 120cm (30 – 48in), and exposed buildings are evacuated. More than 120cm (48in) results in whole villages being put on the alert.

Wind-drifted snow is the most likely to avalanche. It's as if the big slab is in tension; when you cut it, it all comes down. Wind is the main cause of avalanches.

Noise can be an indicator, particluarly the 'whoomph' you hear when one layer sinks and begins to detach itself.

Cracks that spread out ahead of you are bad news.

Spring snow can be very dangerous when the sun has been on it. If you start breaking through, leave the slope immediately.

The following types of snow are unsafe:
• Hoar frost (which forms a very slippery layer).
• Shiny, sun-affected snow.
• Very loose powder snow, particularly if banked up by the wind.
• Crystallised loose snow, which makes air spaces.
• Cup-crystals (big beaker-shaped crystals), especially when they are wet or when the top layer is not firm because the ground is soft. This occurs especially in the spring as the weather becomes warmer.
• Snow is less safe when it cannot be made into snowballs.

Taking a snow profile is informative because you can tell if the layers of snow are sticking to each other properly. I

FLIP

recommend you spend time on a course learning this technique. In the meantime try pushing the basket into the snow. If it disappears into a pocket of air the alarm bells should ring loudly. But the reverse is not necessarily true – firm snow is not always safe.

Basically, to take a snow profile you dig a trench across the fall line, mark out an area as shown below and dig down through the snow layer by layer. As you reach each layer place the shovel in the middle of the 60cm side and pull. The easier the snow slides, the greater the danger of avalanche.

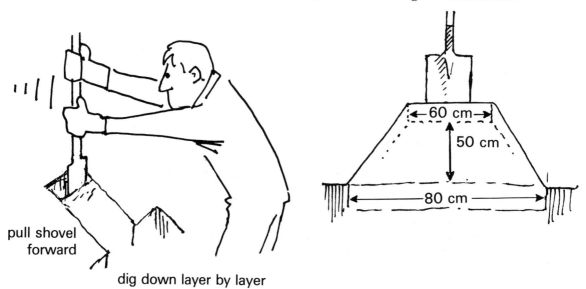

pull shovel forward

dig down layer by layer

60 cm

50 cm

80 cm

OTHER FACTORS

Time of year In the Alps, the avalanche danger is greatest during the first part of February. During March the risk decreases but statistics show a rise in April for the number of avalanche victims, possibly because more people are ski-touring then.

Time of day In spring snow you should always aim to be back before you begin to 'break through'. In any case, if you have an accident late in the afternoon you won't have time to organise a rescue. So don't ski off piste late in the day.

Temperature The temperature of the snow and air at the time of snowfall is important. It may take 20 days for the slopes to be safe after a snowfall at minus 20°C, while it may only take two days for the slopes to be safe after a snowfall at minus 2°C.

TESTING A SLOPE

You may find it helpful to find a short, steep slope that faces in the same direction as the one you're worried about, and test it. If your little slope avalanches, that's a good indicator that you should stay off the big one.

A false sense of security

When you want to ski a slope it's all too easy to persuade yourself that it's safe. Here are a few features people take as safety indicators, which in fact are nothing of the sort.

• Tracks in the snow mean nothing. The person who made them may have been lucky, or snow conditions may have changed since he skied down. I once skied the Saltzegg slope at Wengen for one and half hours with a party, then suspected the conditions were changing and led them to another piste. The very next party down the orginal slope triggered it and were lucky to ski off it before it avalanched.

• Time of day means nothing, but the temperature does. Although in some conditions the morning is safer, avalanches can still happen at any time of day.

• The length of time the snow has been there means nothing. One year I was advising on avalanches for a series of major military manoeuvres in Andermatt. We had

FLIP

dynamited the slopes several times to make sure they were safe, and nothing moved. However, I still had the feeling the snow was unstable. I had the exercises held up while I placed dynamite in what I thought was the crucial spot. The blast and sound waves brought down three avalanches over an enormous area. Yet that snow had been there for weeks, and had originally withstood the effect of tons of dynamite.

Skiing on risky slopes

• Ski beneath rocky outcrops, keeping as close to them as possible. A ridge with no cornice is always the safest place.
• Traverse rapidly from one safe place to another.
• Approach an unsafe slope from the top; *never* traverse it near the bottom.
• Allow only one person to cross the slope at a time.
• If you're really worried move straight down the fall line, taking off your skis if necessary. (That way you won't cut the slope.)

If you are in an avalanche

1. Try to ski out of it by schussing diagonally towards the nearest ridge.
2. Shout so others are aware of what is happening.
3. If you're going to be caught, try to get rid of your poles and skis. Don't use the loops on the poles when skiing off piste.
4. In any case roll *like a bottle* down the slope. Your bindings will release and you will be moving away from the fastest snow, which then has less chance of burying you. The feeling is a bit like rolling up the beach with a big dumping wave behind you. You won't roll straight (your shoulders are wider than your feet) which is helpful as you may well roll out of the side of the avalanche.

5. Keep rolling until you're clear. I was once traversing a gulley with 25cm (10in) of new snow when a big avalanche, starting from a cornice above, hit me really hard. I was swept through the air and finished up at least a kilometre lower down. By rolling I managed to break out and was able to dig out one of my skis and get home on it. I learned a lot in that avalanche: I tried swimming, somersaulting and so on, but rolling was the most effective.

6. The safest route home is over the avalanched snow, as it's unlikely to come down again.

Rescuing someone from an avalanche

1. Watch the person carefully to see where he disappears from view. (If there are several people watching and several people in the avalanche, the watchers should study one person each.)

2. Keep your eyes pinned on the last spot where you saw the victim and send someone else there to mark the spot. (If you try to walk to the place yourself you'll trip over and lose the place.)

3. Time is now of the essence, as the chances of surviving more than 20 minutes buried in the snow are slim.

4. Mark where the tracks enter the avalanche and where the victims were last seen. All skis and other equipment found in the avalanche should be left where they are, having first made sure that no-one is attached to them. Then specialists will be able to reconstruct the incident.

5. Put all your equipment in a safe place.

6. Post someone to watch for further avalanches.

7. Look for other parties who can help.

8. Form up in line, walk a short distance, then stand still and look and listen. Then move forward again.

9. It is better to walk uphill because you can look under the snow blocks.

FLIP

10. Do not hesitate to 'sound' with a ski or a stick if you suspect something.

11. Look hard near obstructions, because avalanche victims are often stopped by them. Indeed, they are usually found near the end or sides of the avalanche, where more snow is deposited.

12. If you have no luck, send two people with a written message to bring a rescue party. Meanwhile the others can carry on the search for the victims.

It is very difficult to predict how long avalanche victims can stay alive when buried in the snow. People have survived six days, while others have died within five minutes, of shock. Just remember two things: speed is essential, and never give up.

5   First aid and rescue

After an accident the ideal way to be rescued is by helicopter. So don't ski off piste when the helicopters are grounded by bad visibility or falling snow.

Major injuries

Usually an accident victim is unconscious or in too much pain to be moved far, so you'll need to send for help. But first move him out of the wind, get him something to lie on and wrap him in as much clothing as possible. Otherwise hypothermia may get to him before the rescue party does. *Never* give him alcohol to drink because this leds to loss of core temperature.

Speed of rescue is now very important: Hypothermia should be treated by experts, and as soon as possible.

If you're in a group of, say, four people, leave one with the victim and send two for help: brief them carefully about where you are, then send them off with a written message (in case they're incoherent when they arrive). You then know exactly the message that will get through.

Ideally they'll make their way to the nearest telephone, perhaps in a house, at the top or bottom of a ski lift, or in an SOS phone box on a road. They should 'phone the police, who will inform the rescue team.

If there are just the two of you, you may have to leave your friend to go for help. But do have a good look around first to find more people. Before you leave mark the spot well with crossed skis, a flag or whatever you can find.

If a helicopter won't be able to fly or land, or if night is falling, you may have to move the victim.

- Try to collect wooden boards or branches to make a sledge.
- If this is impossible you may have to drag him on his back.

Minor injuries

If you have a damaged knee but can still ski in a straight line, come down the mountain in a series of traverses. Make each turn by lying on your back and rolling round, or by taking your skis off and turning round.

But I would hate to end on a gloomy note. Skiing off-piste can lead to accidents, but so can any other worthwhile sport. Skiing through powder, with the snow flying over your head, is one of life's greatest joys. So is tackling a virgin slope, and skiing through trees. Once you've tried them, you'll never want to ski the piste again.

See you out there!

FLIP

Skiing with Martin Epp

If you would like to ski with Martin Epp, contact one of the organisations detailed below. If you are interested in his International Wilderness Training Courses in Lapland or his Canadian Expeditions, contact him direct: Martin Epp, Bergführer, 6490 Andermatt, Switzerland, Tel: 010 41 44 677 33.

Made to Measure Holidays

Made to Measure Holidays operate a variety of Martin Epp off-piste courses and ski tours each year.

OFF-PISTE INSTRUCTION WEEKS
Six days of intensive instruction in off piste technique after which you should be competent enough to tackle one of Martin's Ski Traverses or Ski Mountaineering weeks. Accommodation during the off piste courses is usually in 2-star hotels (halfboard) for the week. Minimum ski standard: 10 weeks skiing and able to ski parallel on piste.

OFF PISTE WEEKS
One week based in a ski resort, skiing the steep and the deep with Martin. Ideal for those who have successfully completed the off-piste course the previous year.

SKI TRAVERSES
You set off on skis (with touring bindings and skins) to traverse an area of the Alps. Uphill walking is kept to a minimum as you use ski lifts where possible, and walk from the top. The longest climb should not exceed 2 – 2½ hours. You ski to a different area each day – the emphasis being on downhill skiing. Accommodation is usually in mountain restaurants.

SKI MOUNTAINEERING
This is the real thing, and you need to be fit before you set out. On these tours you climb on skins (with touring bindings) for anything up to six hours a day. Difficulty of the climb and skiing are graded by Martin – so you can start with an easy tour with climbs which are gentle in the early stages, gradually getting tougher during the week as you become acclimatised. You carry in your rucksack everything you will need for the week.

TELEMARK COURSE
Martin is planning an instructional week in Telemark Skiing, on cross-country Nordic Skis.

For information please write to: Made to Measure Holidays Limited, PO Box 40, Chichester, West Sussex, PO18 8HA. Tel: 0243 533333.

The Ski Club of Great Britain

Martin Epp has worked closely with the Ski Club of Great Britain over many years. The Club's 'Powder weeks' are for skiers to learn or improve their powder skiing in a party of similar standard, skiing together to a mutual aim, and the Club sends a Party Leader in addition to Martin and Serge Lambert. The two 'Powder weeks' are run at the beginning of February at Wengen: one for intermediates and one for advanced skiers.

In addition the Club organises with Martin an 'Off-piste Traverse' from Wengen to Andermatt, where members take small rucksacks, make short climbs each day with the emphasis on the downhill part of the trip as well as the uphill, and stay in mountain hotels and restaurants. This is strongly recommended for keen off-piste skiers wanting a completely new type of holiday.

The Club also runs at least one tour with Martin Epp in a 'Touring Programme', and SCGB members will be able to join the 'High Alpine Training Meet' run in conjunction with the Eagle Ski Club.

You do have to be a Ski Club of Great Britain member, but membership is very reasonable, and can be arranged when booking.

For information please write to: Ski Club of Great Britain, 118 Eaton Square, London, SW1W 9AF. Tel: 01 245 1033.

The Eagle Ski Club

The Eagle Ski Club, in conjunction with the SCGB, organises instructional courses in ski-mountaineering run by Martin. The 'Alpine Training Meet' includes instruction in off-piste skiing and basic ski-mountaineering subjects, especially avalanche safety. The 'High Alpine Training Meet' provides instruction in glacier level techniques including crevasse rescue. Both courses are for two weeks, in March-April, and consist of day-tours and instruction the first week, and a hut-to-hut tour for the second.

For information please write, with s.a.e., to the Eagle Ski Club Hon Touring Sec., c/o Miss E.M. Fulton, 10 Whitefield Lane, Great Missenden, Bucks, HP16 0BP.